Y0-FDT-483

WITHDRAWN

576.5
HAS
1/05

Primary Sources of Revolutionary Scientific Discoveries and Theories™

MENDEL AND THE LAWS OF GENETICS

JOHNSON PUBLIC LIBRARY
274 MAIN STREET
HACKENSACK, NJ 07601
(201) 343-4169

Bogota Public Library
375 Larch Avenue
Bogota, NJ 07603

Heather Hasan

rosen central
Primary Source™
The Rosen Publishing Group, Inc., New York

To my sister-in-law, Tahara. Though we may not share similar genes, you are no less of a sister to me.

Published in 2005 by The Rosen Publishing Group, Inc.
29 East 21st Street, New York, NY 10010

Copyright © 2005 by The Rosen Publishing Group, Inc.

First Edition

All rights reserved. No part of this book may be reproduced in any form without permission in writing by the publisher, except by a reviewer.

Library of Congress Cataloging-in-Publication Data

Hasan, Heather.
Mendel and the laws of genetics / Heather Hasan.— 1st ed.
p. cm. — (Primary sources of revolutionary scientific discoveries and theories)
Includes bibliographical references and index.
ISBN 1-4042-0309-5 (lib. bdg.)
1. Mendel, Gregor, 1822-1881—Juvenile literature 2. Geneticists—Biography—Juvenile literature. 3. Genetics—History—Juvenile literature.
I. Title. II. Series.
QH31.M45H37 2005
576.5'092—dc22

2004006803

Printed in Hong Kong

On the cover: Photograph of Gregor Mendel.

On the back cover: Top to bottom: Nicolaus Copernicus, Charles Darwin, Edwin Hubble, Johannes Kepler, Gregor Mendel, Dmitry Mendeleyev, Isaac Newton, James Watson *(right)* and Francis Crick *(left)*.

CONTENTS

INTRODUCTION The History of Heredity 4
CHAPTER 1 The Father of Genetics 6
CHAPTER 2 Mendel and the Nineteenth Century 15
CHAPTER 3 Experimenting in the Greenhouse 23
CHAPTER 4 The Forgotten Theory 31
CHAPTER 5 Understanding Mendel's Laws 36
CHAPTER 6 How Mendel's Laws Changed the World 47
TIMELINE 52
PRIMARY SOURCE TRANSCRIPTIONS 54
GLOSSARY 56
FOR MORE INFORMATION 58
FOR FURTHER READING 60
BIBLIOGRAPHY 61
PRIMARY SOURCE IMAGE LIST 62
INDEX 63

INTRODUCTION

Genetics is the scientific study of how heredity works. Heredity is the passing of traits such as hair color and height from parents to their children, or offspring. We may never know when people first noticed the existence of heredity. However, archaeologists have found clues that people were domesticating animals and cultivating plants thousands of years ago, which suggests that they knew about heredity.

The History of Heredity

In ancient times, camels, oxen, horses, and dogs were domesticated to serve various roles. People bred horses for speedy transportation and cows for meat or milk. People also developed different kinds of crops—such as wheat, rice, and maize—for food.

Ever since people began cultivating plants, raising livestock, and keeping pets, they have been aware that most offspring tend to resemble their parents. Dogs produce puppies, not kittens. Sunflower seeds grow into sunflowers, not tulips. Evidence suggests that these early people also understood that both good and bad traits are passed down from parents to their offspring. Even the Egyptians and the ancient Hebrews recognized that some diseases are passed down in families.

Ancient people also realized that they could obtain more desirable plants and animals by breeding the best ones together.

Gregor Mendel studied plants that had a variety of features. By comparing the differences, he was able to discover the role genes play in determining a species' appearance. Shown here is a flower called the shadow lady's slipper (*Cypripedium reginae*). This particular shadow lady's slipper has an unusual genetic defect called a double lip, noticeable in the lower section. Physical differences within species were key in Mendel's study of genetics. By recording these unique qualities, he was able to determine which physical traits were passed along from one generation to the next.

They understood the principles of heredity, yet no one really understood how heredity works. In the mid-1800s, however, an enthusiastic and hardworking monk named Gregor Mendel began a quest to answer that very question. With his discoveries, Mendel laid the foundation for the branch of biology that studies genes and heredity. This young branch of biology is now known as genetics, and Mendel is known as its father.

CHAPTER 1

THE FATHER OF GENETICS

Gregor Mendel was born in Heinzendorf, Austria, in a region then known as Moravia. Although the baptismal register shows that Mendel was born on July 20, 1822, it is believed that he was actually born on July 22 of that year. Heinzendorf was a small village of only seventy-two households. Today, this town is known as Hyncice and is part of the Czech Republic.

Mendel was the only son born to Anton and Rosine Mendel. His parents named him Johann, but his name was later changed to Gregor when he became a monk.

Mendel grew up on a small plot of land on which his father grew fruit trees and raised bees. Although the Mendels had little money, they were able to replace their wooden house with a more expensive brick one. They also owned two horses. Part of Mendel's house still stands today, and visitors can see a memorial dedicated to him.

There was plenty for young Mendel to do on the farm to help his father. As a boy, he helped his father farm their land, but he was not destined to be a farmer like his father. It could have been on that farm that Mendel developed his love for science. Perhaps it was while he worked on the farm that Mendel first noticed the pattern of heredity among the livestock.

Gregor Mendel is shown here in this painting working in his garden at the Abbey of St. Thomas in Brünn. Here he conducted breeding experiments with pea plants that helped him discover the statistical laws of heredity. The effects of Mendel's discoveries in genetics are still felt today. As a result of his research, doctors and scientists now understand that traits can be passed from one generation to the next, enabling doctors and scientists to serve a variety of human causes, including the prevention and cure of hereditary diseases. Discoveries in genetics also allow scientists to alter the genes in the foods we eat, changing characteristics such as the rate at which plants and animals grow.

Mendel the Gifted Student

One thing was certain: Mendel loved school. Mendel was lucky that there was a school in his town of Heinzendorf. Many of the other towns in Austria had no schools at all. He began attending the village school as soon as he was old enough. It did not take long for his teachers to notice that he was an exceptionally intelligent boy.

Because he was a gifted student, Mendel's teachers recommended him to an upper elementary school in Leipnik, Moravia (now called Lipnik, part of the Czech Republic). This was a school where exceptional students were sent to prepare them

Gregor Mendel was born and spent the early years of his life in the small town of Heinzendorf, Austria. Heinzendorf looked very much like this illustration of fields in the outskirts of Vienna, Austria, in the mid-eighteenth century. There was abundant farmland and a rich array of plants and animals. Having grown up on a plot of land where his father grew fruit trees and raised bees, Mendel used this variety of plants, animals, and insects to his advantage. It was this abundance of species that would later be key to his interest in the study of genetics.

for the Imperial Royal Gymnasium. The gymnasium was a school that provided an education for the best students, those few who would go on to study at a university. Children who did not attend the gymnasium learned a trade, such as farming or woodworking.

Mendel's parents wanted the best for him. Although they were poor, they managed to scrape up enough money to send him to the gymnasium in 1834, when Mendel was twelve years old.

Mendel's success, however, was hard on his parents, and it was hard on Mendel, too. The gymnasium was in Troppau (now called Opava, located in the Czech Republic), more than 20 miles (32.2 kilometers) from their home. This may not seem very far, but people back then did not yet have cars to get them from place to place. Because the gymnasium was so far from home, Mendel had to live there. This was very expensive, and the Mendels were only able to pay half his expenses. This meant that young Mendel had to live on half the food that he needed as a growing boy. Mendel must have suffered from more than a few hunger pangs, despite the bread and other foods that his parents sent him from their farm whenever they could.

Mendel's parents also had to deal with the fact that Mendel would not be taking over the family farm when his father grew older. In 1838, Mendel's father was seriously injured while working. This situation placed a lot of stress on young Mendel. His parents were no longer able to pay for any of his schooling, leaving him to support himself entirely. Perhaps due to stress or depression, Mendel became quite sick with a mysterious illness and stayed in bed for several months.

On Mendel's résumé that he submitted as part of a job application, he wrote about how difficult it was to know that he was on his own at the young age of sixteen. Mendel decided to study to become a teacher so that he could make money by tutoring while he continued his education.

Mendel in Olmütz

Mendel attended a course at the teachers' seminary in Troppau. He was then able to make a small amount of money tutoring his classmates. He graduated from the gymnasium in 1840, but wanted to continue his education at a university. In order to go to a university, though, Mendel needed to complete two more years of philosophical study. This education included the history of philosophy as well as mathematics. Mendel decided to enter the Philosophical Institute at Olmütz (now Olomouc in the Czech Republic).

Mendel, however, had little money and was unable to find tutoring jobs in Olmütz. Now desperate, Mendel once again took to his bed with illness, this time staying there for a year. This pattern would be repeated throughout Mendel's life whenever he was faced with difficult circumstances.

Mendel's sisters came to his rescue, though. His older sister, Veronica, had married, and her husband agreed to purchase the family farm. This not only provided Mendel with money but also relieved him of his guilt over not taking care of the farm himself. Mendel's younger sister, Theresia, offered him her dowry, the money that had been set aside for her future marriage. Mendel was so grateful to his younger sister that he later supported the schooling of her three sons.

With the money that his sisters had provided, Mendel was able to complete his two-year study at the Philosophical Institute at Olmütz. There he studied religion, philosophy, ethics, pedagogy (the profession of teaching), mathematics, and physics. However, the money was not enough to allow him to fulfill his dream of attending a university. Mendel later wrote in his autobiography that he no longer wanted to have to struggle. Mendel's physics professor at the Philosophical Institute, Friedrich Franz, who was also a priest, urged Mendel to become a monk. Mendel knew that this was the only way he would be able to obtain an education, because monasteries were known to be centers of learning.

Mendel the Monk and Teacher

Mendel requested admission into the Augustinian monastery of St. Thomas in Brünn. In those days, Brünn was the capital of Moravia. Today, Brünn is known as Brno. Friedrich Franz recommended Mendel to the Augustinian abbot, the head of the monastery. In his recommendation, Franz stated that Mendel had been one of his best students. Mendel was accepted, and he joined the monastery in late 1843, at the age of twenty-one. This is when he changed his name from Johann to Gregor, because it was traditional for monks to change their names when they entered the monastery.

Mendel was ordained into the priesthood in August 1847. He was soon assigned various church duties, such as visiting sick patients in the hospital. It quickly became clear that Mendel was not fit for these duties. He became very upset and ill whenever he visited the patients. Mendel also still desperately wanted to teach.

It was obvious that Mendel was better suited to teaching. For this reason, Abbot Napp, the head of the monastery, wrote a letter stating that Mendel would take up a position teaching mathematics and literature at the secondary school in Znaim. Mendel was thrilled with this change. He began teaching in 1849, even though he did not yet have a formal document from a university approving him to do so.

Mendel excelled as a teacher. He made his lessons exciting and easy to understand, and the children loved him. He still needed to pass a teacher's examination, however, if he wanted to continue. But Mendel had no luck in passing the examination. He was very intelligent, but the exam was difficult. Mendel would have had to

On September 7, 1843, at the age of twenty-one, Gregor Mendel joined the Augustinian monastery of St. Thomas in Brünn, shown here in this current photograph. Mendel's physics professor at the Philosophical Institute, Friedrich Franz, recommended him to the head of the monastery. This was fortunate for Mendel. Since the monastery would pay for his university education, becoming a monk was the only way he was able to pursue his studies. It was here where Mendel conducted his research with pea plants and made his groundbreaking discoveries in genetics.

study for several years in order to do well. He tried hard, but he simply did not have the time he needed to prepare due to his full teaching schedule.

Although Mendel was understandably devastated, it is good for us that he did not pass the exam. If he had passed, Mendel probably would have been happy teaching at the Znaim secondary school for the rest of his life. Several generations of students would have gained an excellent teacher, but science would have lost one of its most brilliant discoverers.

The Making of a Brilliant Scientist

After Mendel failed the teaching exam, he returned to Brünn. However, in 1852, he was sent by Abbot Napp to study at the University of Vienna. Napp cared for Mendel and wanted him to gain greater scientific knowledge, no matter what the cost.

Mendel stayed at the university for two years before returning to the monastery. At the University of Vienna, he studied physics, chemistry, zoology (the study of animals), and botany (the study of plants). The time that Mendel spent at the University of Vienna helped make him the brilliant scientist that he was. There, he acquired the techniques and insights of what was then modern science. This was an exciting time for him.

At the University of Vienna, Mendel met some of the best scientists of his time. He attended a class for experimental physics that was taught by the world-famous Austrian physicist Christian Doppler (1803–1853).

Another brilliant physicist at the university was Andreas von Ettingshausen (1796–1878). He was probably the professor who had the greatest influence on Mendel. Ettingshausen was best known for his mathematical way of figuring out all the possible ways of arranging things in a group. Mendel later realized that he could use Ettingshausen's theory to understand how heredity is determined. Mendel thought that he could perhaps calculate the way that hereditary determinants are arranged.

What Mendel learned from his botany professor, Franz Unger (1800–1870), was also important for his future. Unger made a strong impression on Mendel. Unger was one of the most controversial biologists of the time. In his *Botanical Letters* (1852), Unger stated that he believed that the characteristics of plants gradually changed, or evolved, over generations. This went against what the Catholic Church believed at that time. The church stated that nature remained exactly the way it had been originally created by God, as described in the Bible. Because Unger's ideas differed from what the church believed, Unger was threatened with dismissal from the university.

Unger also taught Mendel about another scientist named Matthias Schleiden (1804–1881). Schleiden discovered that all plants and animals are made up of cells. This was also a revolutionary idea at that time. Unger greatly deepened Mendel's interest in botany and inspired him to study heredity in plants.

CHAPTER 2

MENDEL AND THE NINETEENTH CENTURY

During Mendel's time, Brünn was one of the fastest-growing cities in Europe. It had a population of 70,000. The people who lived in Brünn were from many different cultures, and they spoke many different languages. Mendel was very active in the social and cultural life of the town. He was first vice president and then president of the local mortgage bank, the Hypotheque Bank. Mendel was also the founding member of the Austrian Meteorological Society, which studied weather.

Mendel was also elected to committees on education, roads, and agriculture. Brünn was an area that was obsessed with agriculture, the science of farming. Agriculture was vital to Brünn's economy. The townspeople made money by selling the crops they grew. Sheep breeding and the growing of fruit trees and vines were also important in Brünn. This may account for why Mendel was so interested in heredity and why he chose to study plants.

Politics in Nineteenth-Century Austria

Feudalism still existed in the early nineteenth century in the Austro-Hungarian Empire, during which Mendel was born. It did not officially end until 1848. In the political system of feudalism,

Throughout history, science has often been influenced by religion and politics. With Gregor Mendel, this was also the case. In 1807, Emperor Franz I of Austria (1768–1835), pictured here, ordered the Augustinian monks of St. Thomas to take over the teaching of mathematics and religion at Brünn's Philosophical Institute. Franz I was also known as Francis von Habsburg and Francis I. Franz I was the last Holy Roman Emperor, ruling from 1792 to 1806. He ruled Austria from 1804 to 1835. Some of the most revolutionary scientific discoveries, like Mendel's genetics research, have been heavily influenced by religious and political causes. These obstacles have made great scientists, like Mendel, all the more respected in their fields.

there are two classes of people: the nobles and the peasants. The king gave land to his most important nobles, such as his barons and bishops. These people were referred to as lords. The peasants lived and worked on the land of the noblemen. In exchange, the peasants were offered protection from potential invaders.

The village in which Mendel grew up was part of the estates of Countess Walpurga Truchsess-Zeil. It is because of her that Mendel was able to go to school as a young boy. Countess Truchsess-Zeil was interested in educating the children who lived on her estates. Although many other villages did not have schools, Mendel's did. And school was where Mendel's brilliance was first noticed.

In 1848, a revolutionary movement spread throughout Austria. People wanted more civil liberties, such as the right to vote, the right to write whatever they wanted, and the right for workers to go on strike. They also wanted an end to feudal labor. At the time, Mendel was living in the monastery. Although his life was barely affected by the revolution, Mendel did sign a petition demanding full citizenship for monks. Under the feudal system, monks lost all their civil rights when they entered the monastery. The petition that Mendel signed was ignored, but the end of feudalism in Austria was announced on March 13, 1848.

Life in the Augustinian Monastery

Entering a monastery may sound like an unusual thing for somebody to do today, but it was not that unusual in nineteenth-century Austria. Because Austria was still feudal, sons who would not inherit their father's land had few options for making a living. Their only choices were often to join the army or a religious community.

Religious communities, such as the Augustinian monastery of St. Thomas, which Mendel joined in 1843, had several functions. Although prayer and worship were a priority, monasteries also wanted to be self-sufficient. They grew their own food and made liquor, specialty wines, and cheeses to sell to the outside world. Most monasteries also performed services, such as caring for the poor and sick. Monasteries were also often places of intellectual activity.

The Augustinian order was one of the less strict groups of monks. The monastery was more like a college dorm than a religious establishment. This was not true for some other groups of monks at that time. Some groups had very strict

At the time of Gregor Mendel's stay, the monastery, especially the monastery of St. Thomas, was becoming a great institute for science and learning. Realizing the importance of education, the Moravian Catholic Church encouraged intellectuals, like the ones shown in this portrait taken at the Abbey of St. Thomas in Brünn, to aggressively pursue their courses of study. Mendel is shown holding a fuchsia plant among other monks who studied in fields as varied as physics, religion, and music.

rules. In some orders, the monks were even required to live in isolation. These monks were not allowed to speak to or see anyone else.

By contrast, the Augustinians stressed teaching and research over prayer. This was especially true after 1807. In 1807, Emperor Franz I decided that the Augustinian monks of St. Thomas were to take over the teaching of mathematics and religion at Brünn's Philosophical Institute.

It might have initially appeared that Mendel was cutting himself off from the world when he became a monk. For Mendel, however, the opposite was true. Once he became a monk, he no longer had to struggle to survive. He had a roof over his head and food to eat. He also had plenty of time and resources with which to study science. In fact, the Augustinian monastery was known at that time as one of the best places for learning science.

At the beginning of the nineteenth century, people began to realize the importance of science. Even the Moravian Catholic Church shared this feeling. What a great place for a gifted man like Mendel to be! When he entered the monastery, he was encouraged by the empire, the church, and the abbot to study whatever sciences (such as meteorology, physics, botany, and mathematics) he found interesting.

Mendel and the other monks were also fortunate to have all the materials they needed at the monastery. The Augustinian monastery of St. Thomas, like other religious institutions at that time, received money from the local farms. With this money, the monks bought plants to study, scientific instruments, and other useful tools.

Mendel's monastery also had a well-kept library, which contained books on many different subjects. Mendel made good use of the library. Every morning, he got up at six o'clock and went straight there to study. More important, however, Mendel had access to an experimental garden inside the monastery. The original, colored drawings of the plans for the greenhouse still exist today and show its size and shape. It was there that Mendel carried out his experiments and sought to explain the mysteries of heredity.

As a testament to his career in the study of genetics, the Abbey of St. Thomas in Brünn created a museum in Mendel's honor. Located at the abbey, the museum, called Mendelianum, houses the microscope and slides Mendel may have used in his studies, though some accounts say that Mendel never used a microscope throughout his entire career. The library in the background contains the books that Mendel used throughout his research. Included in this library would have been the works of naturalist Charles Darwin, who developed the theory of evolution and the theory of natural selection. Also part of the library would have been the works of Jean-Baptiste Lamarck, the founder of the science of biology.

Biology in the Nineteenth Century

In the early nineteenth century, a scientist by the name of Jean-Baptiste Lamarck (1744–1829) combined the study of plants and animals into one field of science. He called it biology. Lamarck thought of the natural world as a staircase, with every living thing striving to become more complex, moving up the steps of the staircase. How did living things become more complex? Lamarck believed that they reacted to their environment in order to improve themselves.

Furthermore, Lamarck believed that parents could then pass their traits down to their offspring. He even went so far as to say

Shown here is the title page of Jean-Baptiste Lamarck's *Flore Française* (French Flora). Even today, this is a useful manual for plant identification. Lamarck was a major influence on Mendel's life. Lamarck was one of the pioneers of the new science called biology. Biology combined the study of plants and animals into one field. By studying the characteristics of both plants and animals, he treated specimens from all species as if they were the same. And in a sense they were. All living organisms have genes, which they pass down from generation to generation. The genes of plants and animals behave in the same way. Without Lamarck's work, Mendel may not have advanced as far as he did in discovering the nature of genes and heredity.

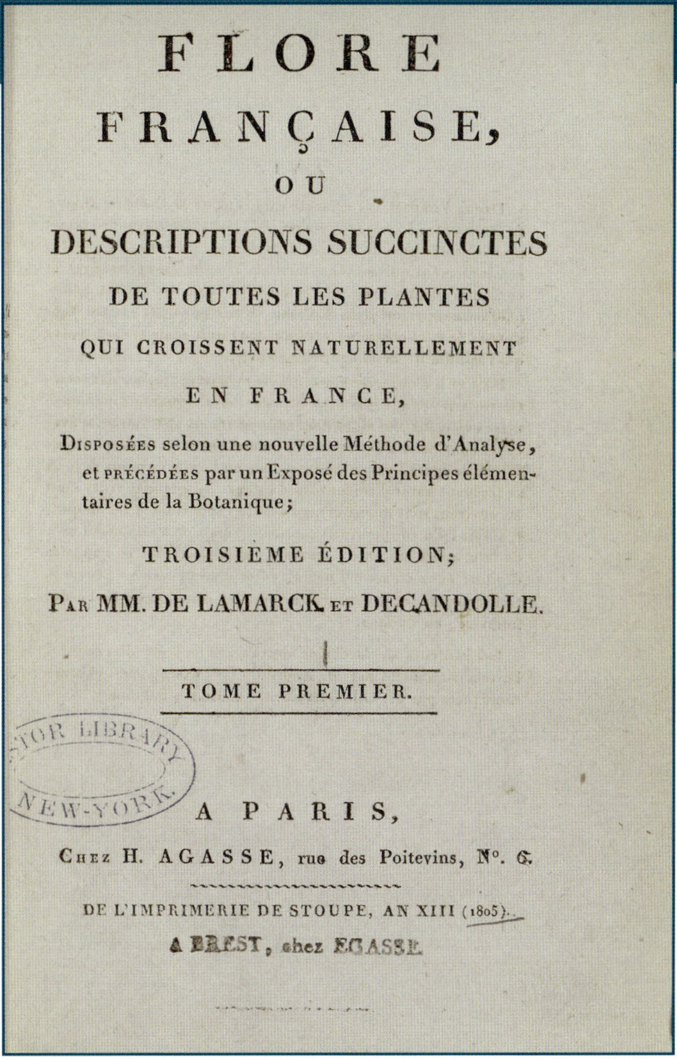

FLORE
FRANÇAISE,
OU
DESCRIPTIONS SUCCINCTES
DE TOUTES LES PLANTES
QUI CROISSENT NATURELLEMENT
EN FRANCE,

Disposées selon une nouvelle Méthode d'Analyse, et précédées par un Exposé des Principes élémentaires de la Botanique;

TROISIÈME ÉDITION;

Par MM. DE LAMARCK et DECANDOLLE.

TOME PREMIER.

A PARIS,
Chez H. AGASSE, rue des Poitevins, N°. 6.

DE L'IMPRIMERIE DE STOUPE, AN XIII (1805).

A BREST, chez EGASSE.

that parents could pass down habits they had formed during their lifetime. Lamarck suggested that these acquired changes gradually turned a species, or specific type of plant or animal, into a new species. These ideas angered the religious leaders of that time. However, no scientist upset them more than Charles Darwin (1809–1882) did.

Darwin was not happy with Lamarck's explanation of how species were formed. Darwin did not believe that the environment produced the variation, or differences, among animals in a population. Darwin believed that the variation between different organisms already existed. He theorized that a process, which he called natural selection, determined which of these different traits would be passed on from one generation of organism to the next. He believed that a certain trait might make one animal more likely to survive than another animal that did not have that trait. An animal with speed may be better adapted to its surroundings by being able to outrun its predators. This animal would then have a better chance of surviving long enough to produce offspring with that same trait. Supporters of Darwin called this competitive process "survival of the fittest." The fittest were those organisms that were most fit to survive in their environments.

Even though an interest in heredity by nineteenth-century scientists, such as Lamarck and Darwin, led to many important theories, there were still questions these theories were unable to answer. Darwin's natural selection explained how variety in a species gradually became fixed traits of that species over the generations. However, he wrongly thought that the different traits of parents were blended in the offspring, like the way color is blended when paint colors are mixed. How heredity actually worked was a mystery to Darwin. Mendel was seeking the answer to that very mystery.

CHAPTER 3

EXPERIMENTING IN THE GREENHOUSE

From the time that Mendel was a young boy on the farm, he had observed how vegetables, fruits, and animals tended to resemble their parents. Mendel disagreed with the scientists of his time, such as Darwin, about how traits are passed on from parents to their offspring. Although Darwin did not know about Mendel's work, Mendel was aware of Darwin's. Mendel read Darwin's books *On the Origin of Species* (1859) and *The Variation of Animals and Plants under Domestication* (1868). He made pencil notes in the margins and on the back covers of his copies of these books.

Mendel agreed with a good amount of what Darwin said, but he did not agree with Darwin's view on heredity. He did not agree that parents' traits are blended when making offspring. Perhaps Darwin's blending theory did not fully explain what Mendel had observed on the farm where he grew up.

Mendel wanted to know how organisms passed on their traits, or features, to their offspring. Why did some traits seem to get passed on while others did not? Did the traits of the parents compete with each other? These were the questions

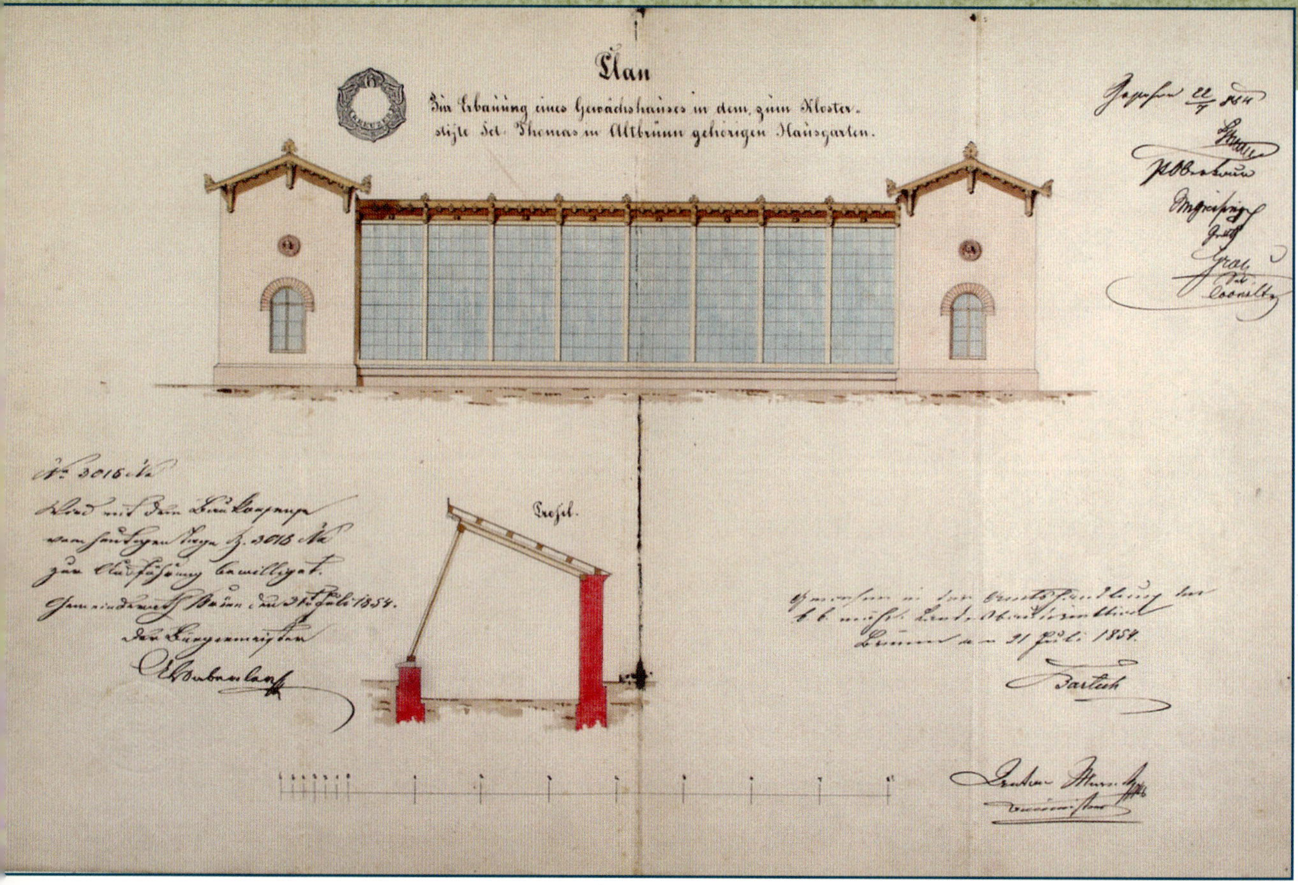

In the Abbey of St. Thomas, Gregor Mendel had access to the glasshouse, or greenhouse, shown here in this 1854 blueprint. In the controlled environment of the greenhouse, Mendel was able to carefully study his varieties of pea plants. Mendel's findings on heredity conducted in this greenhouse did not agree with those of naturalist Charles Darwin, who said that parents' traits are blended when making offspring. The results of Mendel's studies conducted here were the first evidence of the young scientist forming his theories of genetics.

that Mendel sought to answer, and he turned to the garden pea for answers.

Why Garden Peas?

When Mendel returned from the University of Vienna, he found himself overseeing some of the monastery's community food gardens. One of the main crops grown in these gardens was peas. The garden pea, or *Pisum sativum*, as it is called by scientists, was a great organism for Mendel to study for many reasons. For one, the pea plant is very easy to grow. It is also easy to get this plant to interbreed, or breed with another species of plant. In nature, the plant is self-fertilizing and is able to produce offspring without ever coming into contact with another plant. It is able to do this because each plant has both male and female reproductive organs. However, it is easy to crossbreed, or mate different varieties of these plants, in an experiment. The offspring then grow to maturity quickly in a single season.

There were many varieties of peas available to Mendel. In fact, at the monastery today, visitors can still see lists of seeds that Mendel ordered. Many of these self-fertilizing plants produced offspring that were identical to their parents. The different kinds of pea plants differed from each other by the traits they expressed, such as flower color, height, pod shape, and starch content. Mendel decided that he could learn more about inheritance by crossing the different varieties of garden peas. By seeing which traits the offspring of the crosses inherited, he would be able to figure out how traits are passed down from parent to offspring.

Since garden peas mature very quickly, Mendel did not need to wait long to see what kinds of traits his interbred offspring had. In preparation for these experiments, he scribbled comments in his copy of the book *Gärtner's Versuche und Beobachtungen über die Bastarderzeugung im Pflanzenreich* (Gärtner's Experiments and Observations of Hybridization in the Plant Kingdom), which was published in 1849.

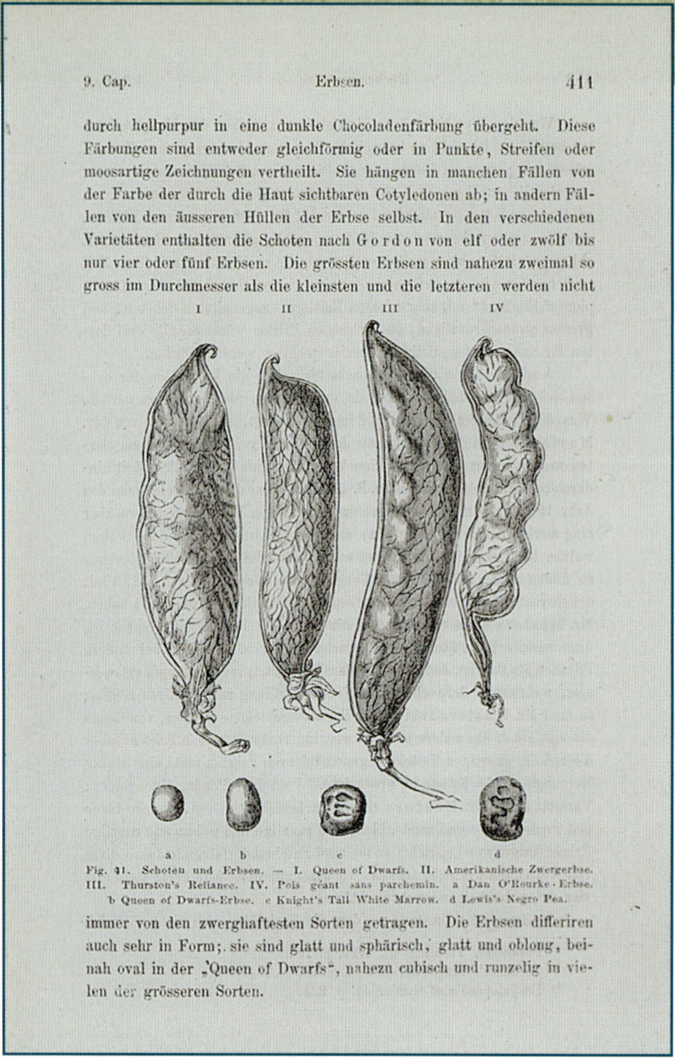

9. Cap. Erbsen. 411

durch hellpurpur in eine dunkle Chocoladenfärbung übergeht. Diese Färbungen sind entweder gleichförmig oder in Punkte, Streifen oder moosartige Zeichnungen vertheilt. Sie hängen in manchen Fällen von der Farbe der durch die Haut sichtbaren Cotyledonen ab; in andern Fällen von den äusseren Hüllen der Erbse selbst. In den verschiedenen Varietäten enthalten die Schoten nach G o r d o n von elf oder zwölf bis nur vier oder fünf Erbsen. Die grössten Erbsen sind nahezu zweimal so gross im Durchmesser als die kleinsten und die letzteren werden nicht

Fig. 41. Schoten und Erbsen. — I. Queen of Dwarfs. II. Amerikanische Zwergerbse. III. Thurston's Reliance. IV. Pois géant sans parchemin. a Dan O'Rourke-Erbse. b Queen of Dwarfs-Erbse. c Knight's Tall White Marrow. d Lewis's Negro Pea.

immer von den zwerghaftesten Sorten getragen. Die Erbsen differiren auch sehr in Form;. sie sind glatt und sphärisch, glatt und oblong, beinah oval in der „Queen of Dwarfs", nahezu cubisch und runzelig in vielen der grösseren Sorten.

Shown here is a page from the naturalist Charles Darwin's *The Variations of Animals and Plants under Domestication*, published in 1868. Darwin was an important figure in Mendel's life. Mendel read Darwin's books on natural selection, which theorizes how organisms evolve. In Darwin's *On the Origin of Species*, the naturalist explains that species evolve by passing the best, or "fittest," traits to their offspring in order to ensure survival. Though Darwin spent his life studying how species evolve, he never figured out how these traits are passed from one generation to the next. Darwin even mistakenly believed that the traits of each parent are blended together in the offspring. (See page 54 for an excerpt.)

Looking for Pure Breeders

Mendel chose seven characteristics of the pea to study. These were the texture of the peas (either smooth or wrinkled); the color of the peas (either yellow or green); the color of the outer coat of the peas (either white or gray); the shape of the ripe, or full-grown, pea pods (plump or wrinkled); the color of the unripe pea pods (either green or yellow); the position of the flowers on the stem of the plants (either all over the stem or bunched at the top of the stem); and the length of the stems (long ones of about seven feet [2.1 meters] or short ones of about one foot [305 millimeters]).

Gregor Mendel developed his theories of genetics by recording the results of his experiments with pea plants. One characteristic of the pea plants that varied from specimen to specimen was color. Mendel crossbred peas that produced yellow (A) and green (B) peas. This produced a generation in which all the peas were yellow (C). In another experiment, Mendel bred the C generation peas together. The result was a mixture of pea colors (D). From these experiments with peas, Mendel came up with his theory for dominant and recessive genes. We learned from Mendel's experiments with dominant and recessive genes that statistics are an important part of the science of genetics.

With the support of Abbot Napp, Mendel began experiments with the pea plants in 1856, in a greenhouse in the monastery garden. Mendel filled the long tables in the glasshouse with pots of pea plants. In each pot, he planted seeds that would grow to show one of the seven traits he had chosen to examine. Like any good scientist, Mendel carefully labeled each pot with the type of seed that was planted in it. That way, he would be certain not to get the pots mixed up.

For two years, Mendel repeatedly planted these same seven types of seeds and watched them grow. He wanted to make sure they were pure breeding. A pure-breeding parent plant always produces offspring that have the same characteristics that it has.

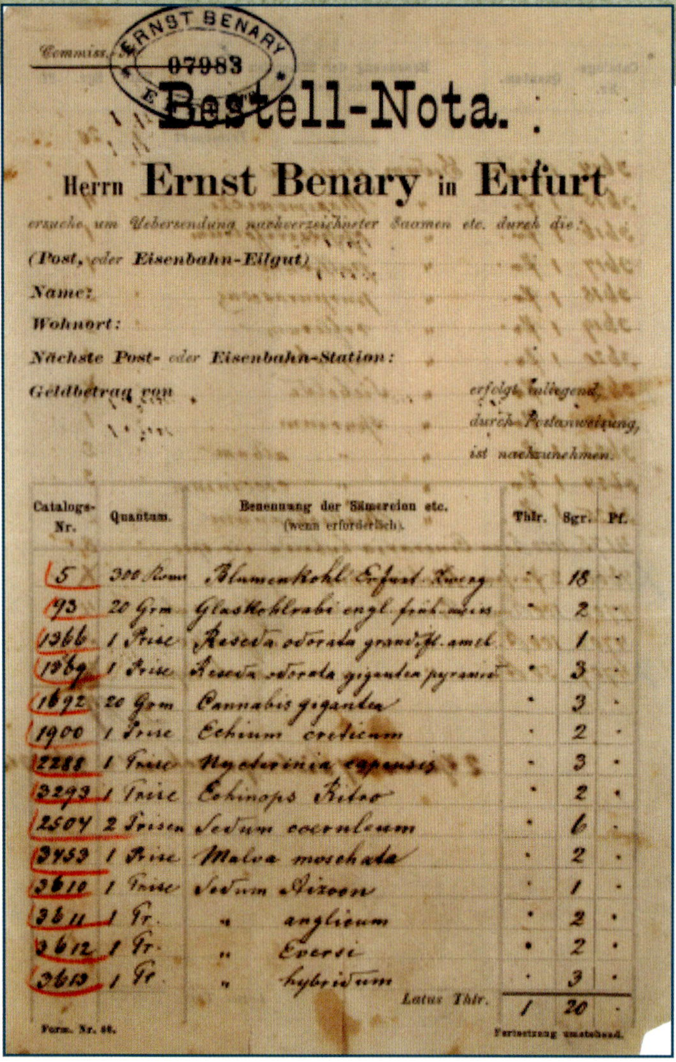

ERNST BENARY

Commiss. 07983

Bestell-Nota.

Herrn Ernst Benary in Erfurt

ersuche um Uebersendung nachverzeichneter Saamen etc. durch die:

(Post, oder Eisenbahn-Eilgut)

Name:

Wohnort:

Nächste Post- oder Eisenbahn-Station:

Geldbetrag von ... erfolgt inliegend, durch Postanweisung, ist nachzunehmen.

Catalogs-Nr.	Quantum.	Benennung der Sämereien etc. (wenn erforderlich).	Thlr.	Sgr.	Pf.
5	300 Korn	Blumenkohl Erfurt Zwerg	·	18	·
93	20 Grm	Glaskohlrabi engl. früh weiss	·	2	·
1366	1 Prise	Reseda odorata grandifl. ameli.	·	1	·
1369	1 Prise	Reseda odorata gigantea pyramid.	·	3	·
1692	20 Grm	Cannabis gigantea	·	3	·
1900	1 Prise	Echium creticum	·	2	·
2288	1 Prise	Nycterinia capensis	·	3	·
3293	1 Prise	Echinops Ritro	·	2	·
2504	2 Prisen	Sedum coeruleum	·	6	·
3453	1 Prise	Malva moschata	·	2	·
3610	1 Prise	Sedum Aizoon	·	1	·
3611	1 Pr.	" anglicum	·	2	·
3612	1 Pr.	" Eversi	·	2	·
3613	1 Pr.	" hybridum	·	3	·
		Latus Thlr.	1	20	·

Form. Nr. 68.

Fortsetzung umstehend.

Shown here is the original copy of a bill from Ernst Benary of the seed firm Bestell-Nota. Mendel bought these seeds from Bestell-Nota on November 2, 1878, to use in his experiments back at the abbey. This record is one of the few records from which we can gain insight into Mendel's work. With such documents as receipts, notebook notations, journal entries, etc., researchers can piece together the life and studies of Mendel.

For instance, seeds from a pure-breeding plant that has wrinkled peas will always produce offspring that have wrinkled peas. He wanted to make sure they were pure breeders so if the offspring had different characteristics in later experiments, Mendel would know where those characteristics came from. Once Mendel was sure that the plants were pure breeders, he was ready to cross, or mate, the different kinds of pea plants together.

Crossing the Plants

Mendel chose to cross, or mate, pea plants that had very different traits. For example, he crossed plants producing round peas with those producing wrinkled peas. In one set of experiments,

Mendel carefully chose a group of pure-breeding tall plants, plants that always produce more tall plants when crossed with each other.

He then crossed these tall plants with pure-breeding short plants. He did this by transferring, by hand, pollen from the tall plants to the short plants. With tweezers, he opened up the part of a plant that holds the pollen and then used a tiny paintbrush to carry the pollen to the other plant. Mendel also used pruning tools to cut off parts of the plants to make them grow better.

Mendel took the seeds that these plants produced and planted them. He named these his first generation of plants (or F1 generation). As the seeds grew into plants, he was able to see which characteristics they had inherited. Would they be tall or short? You might expect that some of the plants would be tall and some would be short, but this is not what Mendel observed. Maybe you think that the offspring would all be medium-height plants since tall and short plants were crossed. Mendel did not observe that either. What did he observe? When the offspring of the tall and short plants grew, Mendel saw that they were all tall!

These tall plants are called hybrids, because their parents had different characteristics, one tall and one short. Although it seemed as though the short trait had disappeared, Mendel soon found that it had not. Mendel allowed the tall hybrids to self-pollinate. When he planted their seeds and allowed them to grow, he found that about one out of every four of the offspring was short. This meant that for every three tall plants that grew, one short plant also grew. This result is known as a 3:1 (three-to-one) ratio. Mendel named these plants the second generation of plants (or F2 generation).

Mendel saw the same pattern with other characteristics. For instance, in another experiment, when he crossed a white-flowered plant with a violet-flowered one, all the first-generation plants had violet flowers. However, if these violet-flowered plants were allowed to self-pollinate, about one-fourth of the second-generation offspring had white flowers.

For eight long years, Mendel worked on his experiments. He worked very hard and crossed thousands of pea plants. Imagine the time it must have taken Mendel to sort, count, and record information about every pea with each different trait. Like any good scientist, Mendel kept careful notes on what he did and what he observed. However, although Mendel attempted to make his observations known, the meaning of his work would go unappreciated until long after his death.

CHAPTER 4

THE FORGOTTEN THEORY

Mendel finally completed his experiments with peas in 1863. In 1865, he presented his results to the Natural History Society in Brünn. His report was so lengthy that he had to go back a second time to finish presenting it.

The society members understood little of what the long-winded monk was saying. In many ways, Mendel was ahead of his time. He had brought the laws of chance and probability to the process of fertilization. Mendel had used his math skills to look for patterns in the results of his crosses. He had counted, for example, that 253 self-fertilized F1 generation plants produced 5,474 round seeds and 1,850 wrinkled seeds. In another instance, he counted 6,022 yellow seeds and 2,001 green seeds in an F2 generation. The numbers would have meant nothing if Mendel had not understood what the statistics meant. Mendel had noted that in all his crosses, the ratio of one trait to the other in the second generation was very close to three to one. This ratio suggested that the makeup of offspring was a matter of chance and was determined by mathematical odds.

Never before had anyone used mathematics to explain biology. Despite their lack of understanding, the society members invited

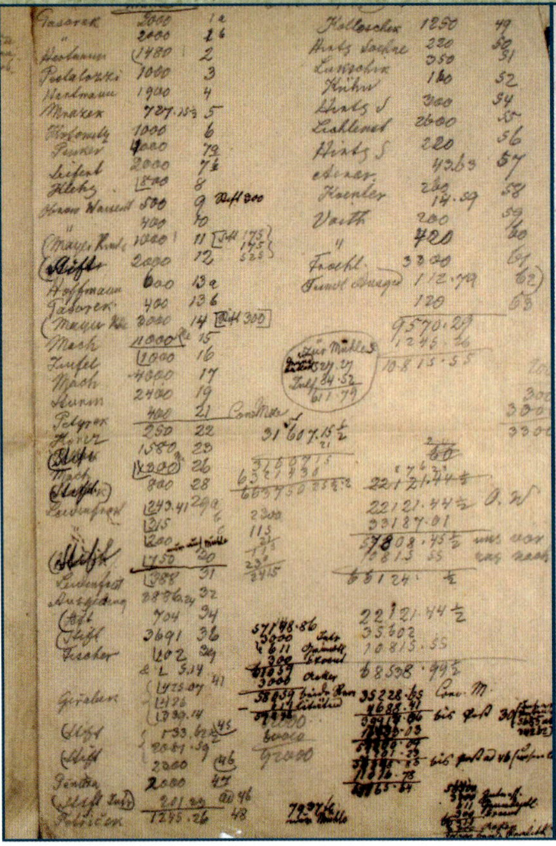

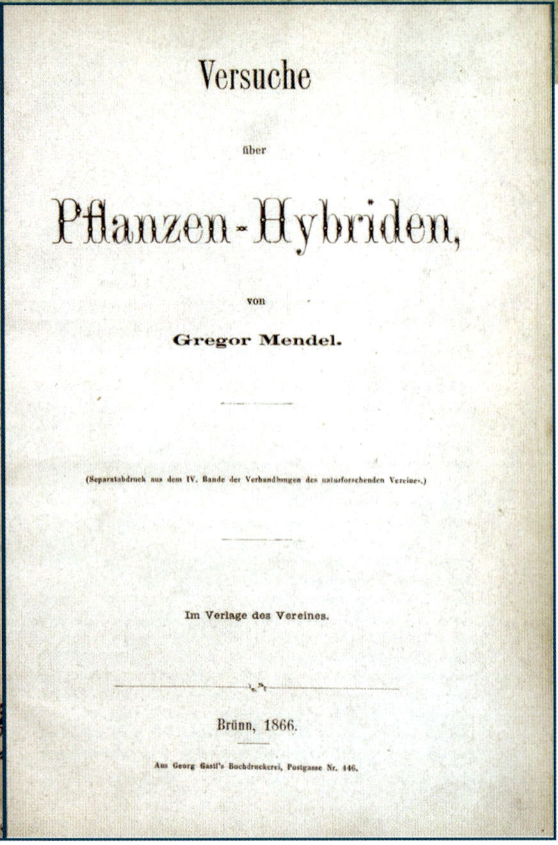

Versuche

über

Pflanzen-Hybriden,

von

Gregor Mendel.

(Separatabdruck aus dem IV. Bande der Verhandlungen des naturforschenden Vereines.)

Im Verlage des Vereines.

Brünn, 1866.

Aus Georg Gastl's Buchdruckerei, Postgasse Nr. 446.

Shown here at left is the notebook Gregor Mendel used to record his results from his crossbreeding experiments with pea plants. The notes explain Mendel's comparison of the results he obtained with *Pisum*, a type of pea, and *Hieracium*, a type of herb, to those obtained with hybrids of *Salix*, which is a type of tree or shrub. The notes also contain a list of names and expenses apparently related to his experiments. These notes would eventually be published in Mendel's paper "Versuche über Pflanzen-Hybriden" (Experiments on Plant Hybridization) on the right. The paper was published in the journal *Transactions of the Brünn Natural History Society* in 1866. (See page 54 for an excerpt.)

Mendel to publish his results in their journal, *Transactions of the Brünn Natural History Society*. Mendel's paper, "Versuche über Pflanzen-Hybriden" (Experiments on Plant Hybridization), appeared in the society's journal a year later, in 1866. Unfortunately for Mendel, the journal in which his paper was published was not widely read.

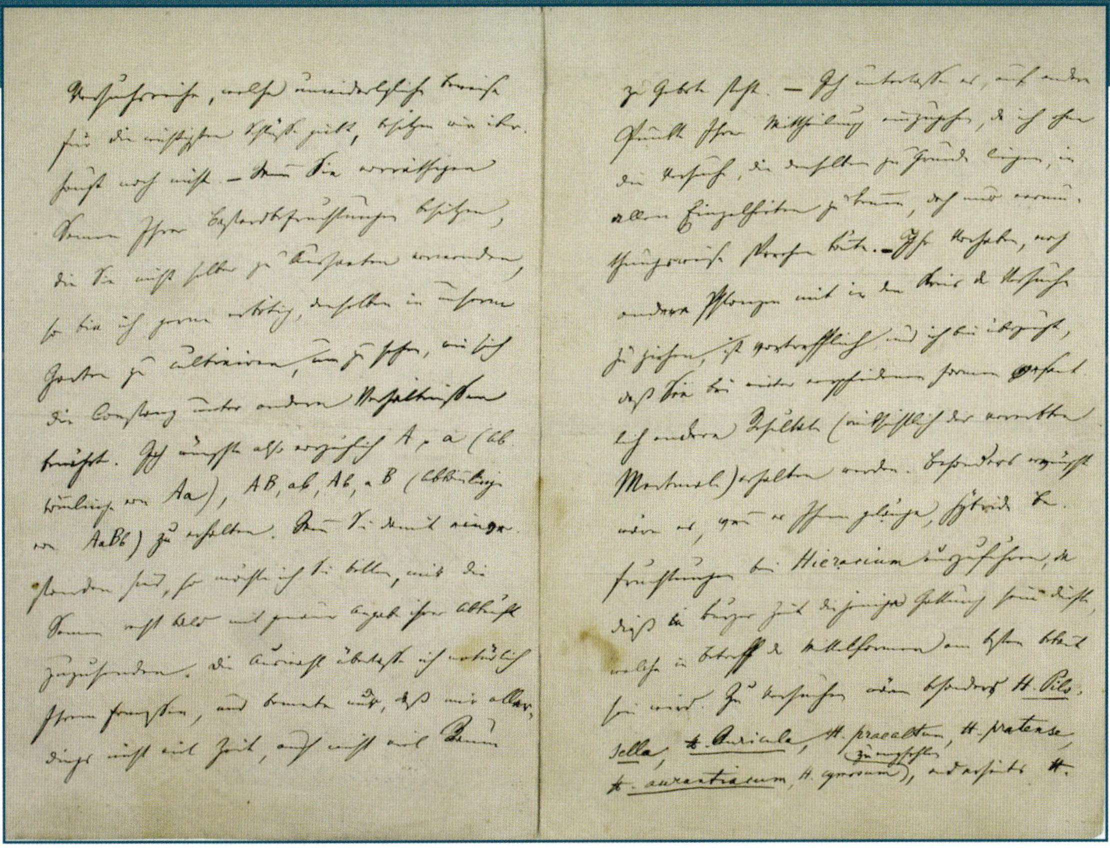

After eight years of crossbreeding his pea plants, Mendel found a mathematical pattern in the results. He published his results in his paper "Versuche über Pflanzen-Hybriden" (Experiments on Plant Hybridization) and sent it to a number of scientists. One of these scientists was a German biologist named Karl Wilhelm von Naegeli. Shown here is a letter of correspondence between Mendel and Naegeli. Naegeli never embraced Mendel's theory. Mendel pushed on and continued to write the esteemed biologist despite Naegeli's skepticism with Mendel's theories. Thanks to Mendel's persistence, we have numerous letters he wrote to Naegeli to use as research into Mendel's life and career. (See page 55 for an excerpt.)

Mendel also sent copies of his paper to many well-known biologists of the time. He waited anxiously for a reply, but his only response came from a German biologist named Karl Wilhelm von Naegeli (1817–1891). Naegeli was one of the most admired botanists of the mid-nineteenth century. Far from encouraging, however, Naegeli's letter of response expressed his doubts of Mendel's ideas.

This may have been disappointing to Mendel, but he continued to write to Naegeli. Much of what we know today about Mendel comes from the letters Naegeli and Mendel wrote to one another. The two men wrote to each other for seven years, but Naegeli never accepted Mendel's findings.

The ultimate irony was that there was one man who would have recognized the importance of Mendel's work right away if he had read it. Charles Darwin knew that the biggest flaw in his theory of evolution was his inadequate theory of inheritance. When Darwin died, a copy of the issue of *Transactions of the Brünn Natural History Society* containing Mendel's paper was found on his bookshelf. However, it had never been opened. He had never read it! Mendel's world-changing discoveries would continue to go unnoticed.

The Tragedy of a Scientist

Mendel was understandably discouraged by the lack of attention that his paper received. He was the first person to understand the importance of applying a knowledge of mathematics to a biological problem. This was a strange idea to the scientists of that time. Mendel may have wondered if his ideas would ever be appreciated.

By 1868, Mendel's contribution to science was finished. In that year, the local newspaper in Brünn announced the election of a new abbot. That new abbot was Mendel himself. As abbot, Mendel was very busy. Although he continued in his interest in bees and fruit trees, he did not have time for further research with his plants. Scientific work became a leisure activity for him.

As an abbot, Mendel became a skilled administrator. He was patient, logical, thorough, and creative. The strengths that Mendel had once used to conduct research in heredity were now being used to govern the men in his monastery. Although the monastery may have gained a hardworking and devoted abbot, the scientific world had lost a brilliant investigator.

As Mendel grew older, his health began to deteriorate. Then, in 1884, when he was just sixty-two, Mendel died of Bright's disease, a chronic deterioration of the kidneys. Although Mendel died well respected by all who knew him, he was as yet unknown as one of the great scientists of the nineteenth century. He would never know that future generations would call him the father of genetics.

The Rediscovery of Mendel

Mendel's work went unrecognized for nearly thirty-five years. It was not until sixteen years after his death that Mendel was finally noticed. At the end of the nineteenth century, three scientists from three different countries began trying to figure out the laws of heredity by doing experiments with plants. These scientists were Hugo De Vries of Holland, Karl Correns of Germany, and Erich von Tschermak of Austria. All three independently reached the same conclusion at the same time in 1900.

However, as they prepared to publish their results, they were surprised and disappointed to find out that a virtually unknown monk had already published a report about heredity. The scientists shared Mendel's work with the world, and he was finally given the credit he was due. From then on, Mendel was known as the father of genetics and his ideas were known as the laws of genetics.

CHAPTER 5

From his findings, Mendel put together some basic laws of heredity. He had sought to discover how the characteristics of plants were passed down from parents to their offspring. Mendel decided that the traits were passed along by what he called heredity factors (today we know them as genes, the basic units of heredity). The heredity factors determined which characteristics the plants would possess. These factors would remain unchanged during the lifetime of the offspring and could then be passed on to the next generation.

UNDERSTANDING MENDEL'S LAWS

Mendel believed that each plant has a pair of heredity factors for each trait—one from each parent. For instance, each plant has two factors for height, two factors for color, two factors for pea shape, and so forth. When the plant's sex cells are made, only one of the factors for each of the traits is included in the sex cell. Mendel brought together the sex cells from two different plants when he transferred the pollen. Each plant's sex cell then offered only one factor for each of the traits.

Since crossing a tall pea plant with a short one produced offspring that were all tall, Mendel knew that heredity was not simply a matter of equally mixing the factors from each parent. If the idea of blending had been correct, Mendel would have gotten all medium-sized plants. To explain the 3:1 ratio that he had discovered, he suggested that one of the heredity factors for a particular trait was dominant, or stronger, than the other factor for that trait. He called the weaker trait "recessive."

Mendel believed that the tall factor was dominant over the short factor. When a plant possessed both a tall and a short factor, the tall factor overpowered the short factor, resulting in an entire generation of tall plants. The short trait had not disappeared, however. It had simply not been visible. The short trait reappeared in the second generation in a plant that had received two short factors. Mendel had discovered what would later be called the laws of genetics.

It's All in the Genes

Mendel made his observations with his naked eyes. In the late 1800s, scientists began using powerful microscopes to help them see tiny things such as cells. All living things are made up of cells. The human body has about 100 trillion cells. The microscope helped scientists see what it is inside the cell that determines heredity.

Scientists found that inside each cell are tiny structures called chromosomes. Each chromosome has even tinier units on it. These units are called genes, which determine the traits that we inherit from our parents.

The chromosomes are found in the nucleus, or control center, of the cell. Every species has a certain number of chromosomes in each of their body cells. You have forty-six chromosomes, a gorilla has forty-eight, and a pea plant has fourteen.

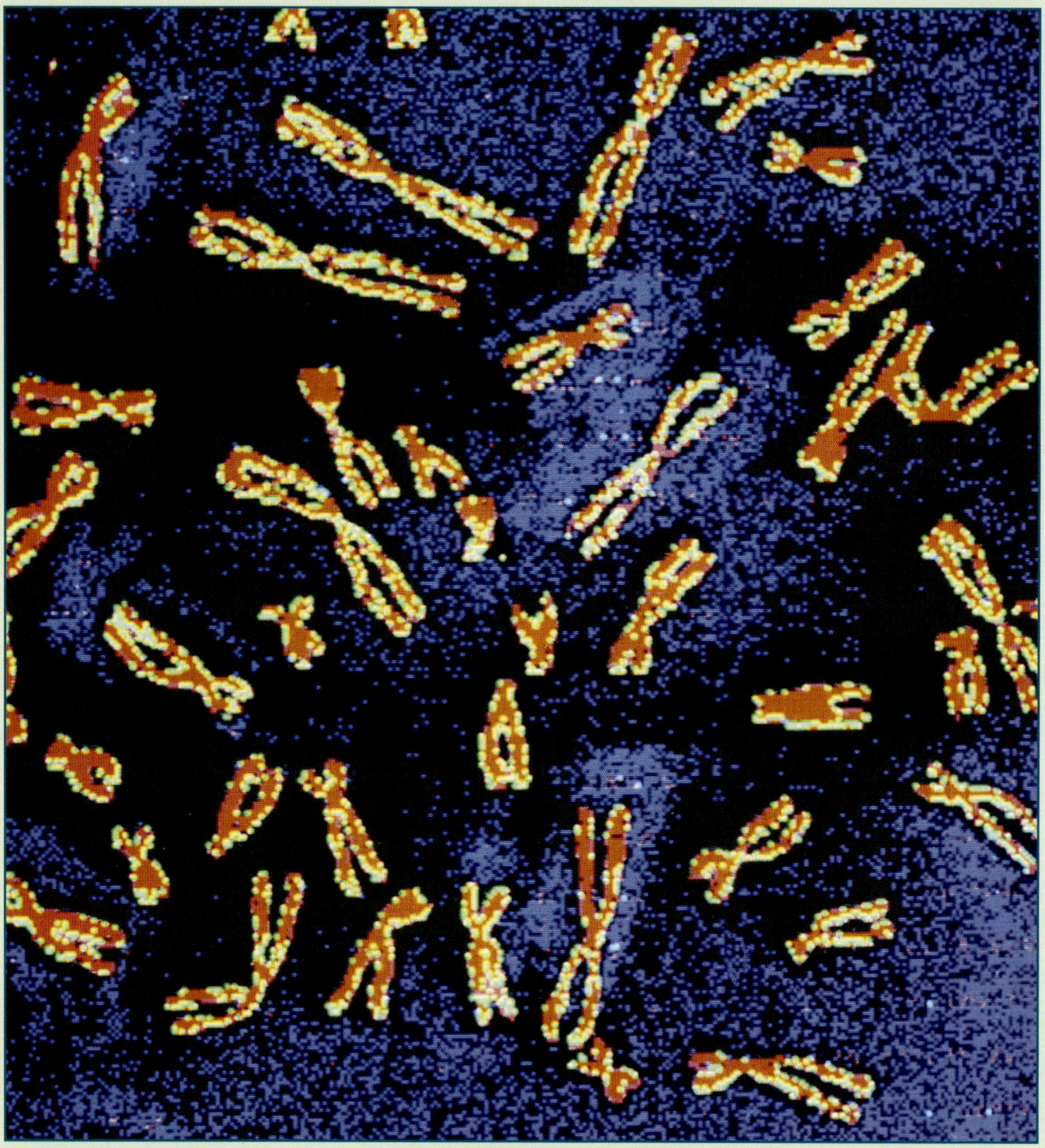

Mendel was not able to see the genes he discovered. He was only able to see the results of the role genes play in life. These results came in the form of various colored pea plants or plants of different heights. Today, with the technology of powerful microscopes, we are able to take a closer look at chromosomes, which contain genes. Shown here is an image of chromosomes.

The number of chromosomes that an organism has in its cells is always an even number. That is because the chromosomes always occur as pairs in the cell. You have twenty-three pairs of chromosomes in each of your cells, making a total of forty-six chromosomes. The pea plant has seven pairs of chromosomes, making a total of fourteen chromosomes.

Each chromosome can have thousands of genes on it. It is because of these genes that you have one brain and two arms. Your genes told your body to grow that way. What color is your hair? Do you have freckles? Do you have big feet? These things were all determined by your genes.

Half from Mom and Half from Dad

You received your genes from your parents. You may look a little bit like each of your parents. That is because one sex cell from your father joined with a sex cell from your mother to make you. Sex cells are different from the other cells in the body. They have half the number of chromosomes as the rest of the cells, only one chromosome from each pair. The sex cells in your body have only twenty-three chromosomes. When your parents' sex cells joined to make you, you received twenty-three chromosomes from each of them. Nearly all the cells in your body have twenty-three pairs of chromosomes, for a total of forty-six chromosomes in each cell. One chromosome of each pair came from your mom, while the other chromosome came from your dad.

The plants that Mendel worked with had sex cells, just as humans do. When Mendel transferred pollen from one plant to another, he was bringing together the sex cells of the two plants. Each plant's sex cell has seven chromosomes, so the resulting

Gregor Mendel showed us that the traits of all organisms are passed from one generation to the next. This image shows the human reproductive process of a female egg being surrounded by sperm. The offspring will inherit half the genes from the male and half the genes from the female. As a result, the baby will be born with some of the father's characteristics and some of the mother's. Traits are passed this way from one generation to another in all species, not just humans. Because of this transference of traits, all species adapt to their environments. This adaptation, or evolution as Charles Darwin introduced it, is key to the survival of life on Earth.

pea plants all had seven pairs of chromosomes, for a total of fourteen chromosomes in each cell.

Different Forms of Genes

For the plants that Mendel worked with, a single gene controlled a single trait. For example, one gene was responsible for flower color, another for plant height, and another for seed shape. There may be several different versions of a gene, however. One version of the gene for plant height might result in a tall plant, while another version might result in a short one. The different forms, or versions, of genes are now called alleles.

Mendel discovered that the gene for plant height had two alleles (though he did not use that name)—one tall allele and one short allele. He also saw that the gene for flower color had at least two alleles. One allele was for white and one allele was for violet. When Mendel crossed two plants, a copy of only one allele of each gene was passed from each parent. The offspring got only one allele for each trait from each parent. Since the offspring got one allele from each parent, it ended up having two alleles for each trait, just like its parents.

Just like the pea plants, you received two genes for each of your traits. One of the alleles from the pair came from your mother's set of chromosomes and one from your father's. In your cells, you have multiple alleles for eye color, for hair color, for height, and so on. These alleles may be the same, or they may be different. Even though your body may have multiple alleles for eye color, it will only show the one that is dominant.

Dominant vs. Recessive

Mendel argued that each plant carries two copies of the genes that determine shape, color, or height. However, he believed that one is dominant, or strong, while the other is recessive, or weak. Only the dominant allele of the gene will be expressed. A dominant allele hides the effects of a recessive allele. For his plants, Mendel found that the allele for purple flowers was dominant over the allele for white flowers. If a plant had received a purple-flower allele from one parent and a white-flower allele from the other parent, the plant would have purple flowers. The only way that a plant could have white flowers is if it had received white-flower alleles from both of its parents. That way, there would not be a stronger, purple allele to mask the weaker, white one.

The reason that Mendel saw all tall plants in the first generation when he crossed tall and short plants was because the tall allele is dominant over the short allele. In the second generation, a 3:1 ratio (three tall plants for every short plant) was seen. This showed that the short allele had been there all along. It was only able to be expressed, however, when the plant had received two short alleles.

In people, the allele for brown eyes is dominant, while the allele for blue eyes is recessive. If a child receives an allele for blue eyes from one parent, but an allele for brown eyes from the other parent, that child will have brown eyes. The only way the child could have blue eyes would be if he or she had received blue-eyed alleles from both his or her parents.

Beyond Mendel

Inheritance in most organisms, however, is much more complex than Mendel thought. Since his time, scientists have discovered that alleles are not always dominant or recessive. Sometimes, the two alleles can compromise to produce something in between. An example is when red snapdragons are crossed with white snapdragons, resulting in all pink snapdragons in the first generation.

These results do not prove the blending theory, however. The blending theory says that the red and white traits would not be

An example of how complex genetics can be, these snapdragons prove that genes are not always dominant or recessive, and can sometimes mix. With this species of plant, red and white snapdragons do not produce either red or white offspring when crossed. Instead, they produce a mixture including red, white, pink, yellow, and orange snapdragons, as shown here. This blending of traits was not predicted by Mendel and would suggest that Mendel's theory of dominant and recessive genes was wrong. However, red and white genes show up in later generations of snapdragons, showing that the traits do not blend.

seen again in later generations but would continue to blend until all snapdragons were pink. However, we know that the red and white alleles show up in the snapdragons in later generations.

We also now know that there are instances when two alleles are both fully expressed. This is seen with blood type. Sometimes, there are also more than two different alleles for a certain gene. For example, the gene for fur color for a mouse may have alleles for black, brown, gray, or white. Only two of these alleles would be involved in the cross, but they would come from a possible four.

Soon after Mendel was rediscovered, scientists also realized that traits are often controlled by more than one gene. Although each of the pea plant traits that Mendel examined were indeed controlled by only one gene, we now know that many traits are controlled by two or more genes. This is the case for most human traits, such as skin color. Skin color is determined by the pigment melanin. Each person has two gene pairs (four alleles) that control the production of melanin. This results in skin colors ranging from very light to very dark. Although there have been additions to Mendel's laws, his laws have definitely stood the test of time.

We Are All Unique

Humans have about 50,000 different genes. Almost all these genes have at least two alleles. Even though family members may resemble each other, none of them looks exactly alike because there are so many different ways that genes can be combined. Mendel stated that allele pairs separate when forming sex cells. Alleles then randomly come together when the male and female sex cells combine during fertilization. It is like tossing coins, drawing cards, or rolling dice. The number of possible combinations is almost endless!

Even though there are more than 5 billion people on Earth, no two people look exactly alike, except for identical twins. Identical twins result when a fertilized egg divides, but the two halves do not stick together. Each half goes on to develop into a baby. Since both babies come from the same egg, they have

Because genes are combined in countless ways when passed from generation to generation, there is a great variety of differences from organism to organism. These organisms include people, too. Aside from identical twins, we each have a unique appearance. And even though identical twins may look the same, their personalities are different. No two people in the world are identical.

Queeny, a six-month-old Persian and Siamese cat, is proof that each individual organism within a species is unique. Queeny's two different colored eyes are not characteristic of her species. However, the specific genes she inherited from her mother and father gave her this unique look. Queeny is an example of how genetics can produce unexpected outcomes in certain offspring. These differences in organisms were essential to Mendel. By tracking the different characteristics in offspring, Mendel was able to track which traits were passed from one generation to the next. As with the multicolored pea plants, Mendel was able to use this unique outcome to support his theory of genetics. As for Queeny, vets say that she has perfect vision.

the same exact genes. They look exactly alike! If you are not an identical twin, there is no one else who looks exactly like you. People may tell you that you have your mother's eyes, but you are unique!

CHAPTER 6

HOW MENDEL'S LAWS CHANGED THE WORLD

Mendel's discovery marked the beginning of a quest to understand how inheritance works. Once Mendel's laws were rediscovered, they gained rapid acceptance and led to many other discoveries.

In 1908, it was suggested that Mendel's particles be called genes, a Greek word that means "to give birth." By 1915, Thomas Hunt Morgan had discovered that genes were arranged on chromosomes. By 1944, it was determined that genes are a sequence of deoxyribonucleic acid (DNA), the code that programs all living things. By 1953, James Watson and Francis Crick had come up with the structure of DNA. Since then, many more exciting advances have been made in the field of genetics. Our knowledge of genetics now helps us to do things such as breed plants and animals, and to understand and treat illnesses.

Understanding and Treating Illnesses

When Mendel discovered the laws of genetics, he started a process that, today, helps us to understand and treat diseases. Many diseases are known to be inherited. Scientists can now

Scientists have come a long way since Mendel's study of genetics. Gene therapy, or the curing and preventing of diseases through gene manipulation, has become a popular new technology. Shown here is an X-ray of bands of human DNA fragments. The black bands reveal the DNA sequence of the genes. By being able to read these bands, doctors are able to determine which genes may cause diseases in an individual. Scientists have also been able to use gene therapy to change the characteristics of the foods we eat. This is called genetic modification. There is a lot of controversy surrounding genetic modification of food. Critics say that altering the genes can make the foods we eat unsafe.

determine whether a person is likely to pass on certain diseases to their children, such as cystic fibrosis, a disease that causes lung and digestive problems, or Huntington's disease, which affects the brain.

Researchers are looking for ways to replace the genes that cause genetic illnesses. This is called gene therapy. In 1990, a four-year-old girl named Ashanthi DeSilva became the first person to receive gene therapy. She had a rare inherited condition called ADA deficiency, which prevents babies from developing their own immune system. Even a common illness can kill a child with this condition. Doctors injected healthy genes into her body to make her better.

Gene therapy allows scientists to prevent and cure diseases like never before. Six-year-old Ashanthi DeSilva, shown here, is living proof of the success of gene therapy. DeSilva suffers from ADA deficiency. ADA deficiency is a rare disease of the immune system. It prevents babies from developing their own immune system, which fights off illness. ADA deficiency usually results in an early death for the sufferer, but for DeSilva, gene therapy helped save her life.

Scientists are always searching for new gene-based drugs to treat diseases such as Alzheimer's, which causes memory loss; multiple sclerosis, a disease of the brain and spinal cord; and Parkinson's, which affects the nervous system. None of this would be possible if the laws of genetics had not been discovered.

Breeding Plants and Animals

Today's scientists have gone well beyond what even the most skilled farmers can do with plants and animals. They have

Gregor Mendel is known as the father of genetics. Because of his experiments with pea plants, among other species, we now understand how traits are passed from one generation to the next. It was because of Mendel's early experiments that we've reached the point that we have in the study of the science. As a testament to his great work, this statue of Mendel was placed in the garden of the Mendel Museum of Genetics at the Abbey of St. Thomas in Brno, Czech Republic, where it all began.

learned how to change the ways that genes are passed on from parents to their offspring. This helps to improve our lives, and it also makes our lives more convenient.

One example of how our lives are improved is the way that scientists are able to modify plants and animals so that they grow more quickly. Now we do not need to wait as long before an animal is big enough to be used as food. Scientists even believe that they have found a way to put certain fish genes into cows, adding the nutritional value of fish to beef.

Scientists can also use their knowledge of genetics to modify our crops so that plants have the traits we desire. They are able to make tomatoes that do not spoil as quickly. They even have the knowledge to make glow-in-the-dark houseplants so that when you get up during the night, you won't stub your toes!

Altering the genes of plants and animals is called genetic modification. Since genetic modification is still new, there is a lot of controversy over whether it is safe and necessary. Tampering with nature may bring unwanted results. Only time and further research will tell whether genetic modification is a science worth pursuing.

These and many other valuable and interesting discoveries have been made in the field of genetics in recent times, but it all started in a monastery garden where a brilliant monk named Gregor Mendel discovered the laws of genetics.

TIMELINE

1822 — Mendel is born in Heinzendorf, Austria.

1833 — Mendel goes to school in Leipnik, Moravia.

1834 — Mendel enters the Imperial Royal Gymnasium in Troppau.

1840 — Mendel graduates from the gymnasium in Troppau.

1841 — Mendel studies at the Philosophical Institute at Olmütz.

1843 — Mendel joins the Augustinian monastery of St. Thomas in Brünn. Mendel's first name is changed from Johann to Gregor.

1847 — Mendel is ordained into the priesthood.

1849 — Mendel begins teaching at the secondary school at Znaim.

1852 — Mendel enters the University of Vienna.

1856 — Mendel begins his heredity experiments with pea plants in the garden of the Augustinian monastery.

1863 — Mendel completes his experiments with the peas.

1865 — Mendel presents his findings to the Natural History Society in Brünn.

1866 — Mendel's paper, "Versuche über Pflanzen-Hybriden" (Experiments on Plant Hybridization), appears in the journal of the Natural History Society.

1868 — Abbot Napp dies and Mendel is elected to be the new abbot of the monastery in Brünn.

1884 — Mendel dies.

1900 — Hugo De Vries, Karl Correns, and Erich von Tschermak rediscover Mendel and his work.

PRIMARY SOURCE TRANSCRIPTIONS

Page 26: From *The Variations of Animals and Plants under Domestication*

The first and chief point of interest in this chapter is, whether the numerous domesticated varieties of the dog have descended from a single wild species, or from several. Some authors believe that all have descended from the wolf, or from the jackal, or from an unknown and extinct species. Others again believe, and this of late has been the favourite tenet, that they have descended from several species, extinct and recent, more or less commingled together. We shall probably never be able to ascertain their origin with certainty. Paleontology does not throw much light on the question, owing, on the one hand, to the close similarity of the skulls of extinct as well as living wolves and jackals, and owing, on the other hand, to the great dissimilarity of the skulls of the several breeds of the domestic dogs. It seems, however, that remains have been found in the later tertiary deposits more like those of a large dog than of a wolf, which favours the belief of De Blainville that our dogs are the descendants of the single extinct species. On the other hand, some authors go so far as to assert that every chief domestic breed must have had its wild prototype. This latter view is extremely improbable: it allows nothing for variation; it passes over the almost monstrous character of some of the breeds; and it almost necessarily assumes that a large number of species have become extinct since man domesticated the dog; whereas we plainly see that wild members of the dog-family are extirpated by human agency with much difficulty; even so recently as 1710 the wolf existed in so small an island as Ireland.

Page 32: From "Versuche über Pflanzen-Hybriden"

Experience of artificial fertilization, such as is effected with ornamental plants in order to obtain new variations in color, has led to the experiments which will here be discussed. The striking regularity with which the same hybrid forms always reappeared whenever fertilization took place between the same species induced further experiments to be undertaken, the object of which was to follow up the developments of the hybrids in their progeny.

To this object numerous careful observers, such as Kölreuter, Gärtner, Herbert, Lecoq, Wichura and others, have devoted a part of their lives with inexhaustible perseverance. Gärtner especially in his work *Die Bastarderzeugung im Pflanzenreiche*, has recorded very valuable observations; and quite recently Wichura published the results of some profound investigations into the hybrids of the Willow. That, so far, no generally applicable law governing the formation and development of hybrids has been successfully formulated can hardly be wondered at by anyone who is acquainted with the extent of the task, and can appreciate the difficulties with which experiments of this class have to contend. A final decision can only be arrived at when we shall have before us the results of detailed experiments made on plants belonging to the most diverse orders.

Those who survey the work done in this department will arrive at the conviction that among all the numerous experiments made, not one has been carried out to such an extent and in such a way as to make it possible to determine the number of different forms under which the offspring of the hybrids appear, or to arrange these forms with certainty according to their separate generations, or definitely to ascertain their statistical relations.

It requires indeed some courage to undertake a labor of such far-reaching extent; this appears, however, to be the only right way by which we can finally reach the solution of a question the importance of which cannot be overestimated in connection with the history of the evolution of organic forms.

The paper now presented records the results of such a detailed experiment. This experiment was practically confined to a small plant group, and is now, after eight years' pursuit, concluded in all essentials. Whether the plan upon which the separate experiments were conducted and carried out was the best suited to attain the desired end is left to the friendly decision of the reader.

Page 33: From Mendel's letter to Naegeli, December 31, 1866

Highly Esteemed Sir:

The acknowledged pre-eminence your honor enjoys in the detection and classification of wild-growing plant hybrids makes it my agreeable duty to submit for your kind consideration the description of some experiments in artificial fertilization. The experiments, which were made with different varieties of *Pisum*, resulted in the offspring of the hybrids forming curious series, the members of which, in equal measure resembled the two original types. The presence of non-variant intermediate forms, which occurred in each experiment, seems to deserve special attention . . . In the projected experiments with species of *Cirsium* and *Hieracium* I shall be entering a field in which your honor possesses the most extensive knowledge, knowledge that can be gained only through many years of zealous study, observation, and comparison of the manifold forms of these genera in their natural habitat. For the most part I lack this kind of experience because the press of teaching duties prevents me from getting into the field frequently, and during the vacations it is too late for many things. I am afraid that in the course of my experiments, especially with *Hieracium*, I shall encounter many difficulties, and therefore I am turning confidently to your honor with the request that you not deny me your esteemed interest when I need your advice.

With the greatest esteem and respect for your honor, I subscribe myself,

Gregor Mendel
Monastery capitular and
teacher in the high school.
Brünn, 31 December 1866

GLOSSARY

allele A different form or version of the same gene.

Augustinian monastery A monastery observing the writings of St. Augustine (354–430), a church father and philosopher.

breed A particular species or variety of organism.

cell The basic unit that makes up living things.

chromosome A body found in the nucleus of a cell that contains both DNA and genes.

domestication The training or adapting of animals to human society.

dominant gene A gene that is stronger and is expressed over a recessive gene.

evolution The theory that current species of organisms adapted to their environments through a process of gradual change.

fertilization The joining together of male and female sex cells, resulting in a cell containing two sets of chromosomes, one from the male and one from the female.

gene The specific unit that determines heredity.

gene therapy The treatment of certain disorders by introducing other genes into the patient's cells.

genetics The study of genes and heredity.

heredity The passing of traits from parents to their offspring.

hybrid The offspring of parents from two different species or variety of species.

interbreed To breed together two different organisms, usually from different species.

mate To bring together a male and female organism, resulting in fertilization.

monastery A community of monks.

monk A man living in a religious community under a religious order.

nucleus The control center of a cell, which contains genes, chromosomes, and DNA.

offspring An organism produced from the mating of two organisms.

organism A creature living by the function of its organs.

pollen A grain that contains the male sex cells of a plant.

recessive gene The gene that is weaker than the dominant gene, and which is not expressed when paired with a dominant gene.

species A group of organisms that have certain permanent traits in common.

statistics The mathematics of collecting, organizing, and interpreting numbers.

FOR MORE INFORMATION

Mendel Museum of Genetics
Abbey of St. Thomas
Brno, Czech Republic
Web Site: http://www.mendel-museum.org

The Moravian Museum
Zelny trh6
659 37 Brno, Czech Republic
Web site: http://www.mzm.cz/Default-en.htm

Museum of Science and Industry
57th Street and Lake Shore Drive
Chicago, IL 60637-2093
(773) 684-1414
Web site: http://www.msichicago.org

The University of Arizona
The Biology Project
Department of Biochemistry and Molecular Biophysics
Biological Sciences West
1041 East Lowell Street
P.O. Box 210088
Tucson, AZ 85721-0088
(520) 621-9185
Web site: http://www.biology.arizona.edu/DEFAULT.HTML

Web Sites

Due to the changing nature of Internet links, the Rosen Publishing Group, Inc., has developed an online list of Web sites related to the subject of this book. This site is updated regularly. Please use this link to access the list:

http://www.rosenlinks.com/psrsdt/melg

For Further Reading

Brown, Fern G. *Hereditary Diseases*. New York: Franklin Watts, 1987.

Brynie, Faith Hickman. *Genetics & Human Health*. Milford, CT: The Millbrook Press, 1995.

Edelson, Edward. *Gregor Mendel and the Roots of Genetics*. New York: Oxford University Press, 1999.

Henig, Robin Marantz. *The Monk in the Garden: The Lost and Found Genius of Gregor Mendel, the Father of Genetics*. Boston: Houghton Mifflin Company, 2000.

Klare, Roger. *Gregor Mendel: Father of Genetics*. Springfield, NJ: Enslow Publishers, 1997.

Olby, Robert C. *Origins of Mendelism*. New York: Schocken Books, 1966.

BIBLIOGRAPY

Aaseng, Nathan. *Genetics: Unlocking the Secrets of Life*. Minneapolis: The Oliver Press, Inc., 1996.

Edelson, Edward. *Gregor Mendel and the Roots of Genetics*. New York: Oxford University Press, 1999.

Henig, Robin Marantz. *The Monk in the Garden: The Lost and Found Genius of Gregor Mendel, the Father of Genetics*. Boston: Houghton Mifflin Company, 2000.

Snedden, Robert. *The History of Genetics*. New York: Thomson Learning, 1995.

Sootin, Harry. *Gregor Mendel: Father of the Science of Genetics*. New York: The Vanguard Press, 1959.

PRIMARY SOURCE IMAGE LIST

Cover: Photograph of Gregor Mendel by James King-Holmes.
Title Page: Print of *Pisum sativum*, circa 1790
Page 7: Painting of Gregor Mendel titled *Gregor Mendel at work in His Genetic Strain Garden*, circa 1800.
Page 8: *View of Fields in the Outskirts of Vienna*, circa 1730.
Page 12: A mid-twentieth century photograph of the Abbey of St. Thomas.
Page 16: Painting titled *Emperor of Austria Frances Joseph I in Uniform*.
Page 18: Photograph of Mendel with Augustinian friars at the Abbey of St. Thomas, housed at the Mendel Museum of Genetics in Brno, Czech Republic.
Page 20: Photograph of the Mendel Museum of Genetics by James King-Holmes.
Page 21: Title page of *Flore Francaise* by Jean-Baptiste Lamarck, housed in the New York Public Library.
Page 24: Building plans for the glasshouse in the Abbey of St. Thomas. Housed in the Mendel Museum of Genetics in Brno, Czech Republic.
Page 26: Page from *The Variations of Animals and Plants under Domestication* by Charles Darwin, 1868. Housed in the Mendel Museum of Genetics in Brno, Czech Republic.
Page 28: List of seeds ordered by Mendel from the Bestell-Nota seed firm. Housed in the Mendel Museum of Genetics in Brno, Czech Republic.
Page 32 (left): Mendel's paper and notes, Housed in The Mendel Museum of Genetics in Brno, Czech Republic.
Page 32 (right): Title page to "Versuche über Pflanzen-Hybriden" (Experiments on Plant Hybridization) by Gregor Mendel, published in *Transactions of the Brünn Natural History Society* in 1866. Housed in the Mendel Museum of Genetics in Brno, Czech Republic.
Page 33: Letter from Karl Wilhelm von Naegeli to Gregor Mendel on February 25, 1867. Housed in the Mendel Museum of Genetics in Brno, Czech Republic.

INDEX

A

ADA deficiency, 48
alleles, 41–44
Alzheimer's disease, 49

B

blending theory, 22, 23, 36–37, 42–44
Botanical Letters, 14
Bright's disease, 35
Brünn, 11, 13, 15, 31

C

chromosomes, 37–40, 41, 47
Correns, Karl, 35
Crick, Francis, 47
cystic fibrosis, 48

D

Darwin, Charles, 21–22, 23, 34
DeSilva, Ashanthi, 48
De Vries, Hugo, 35
DNA (deoxyribonucleic acid), 47
dominant genes, 37, 41–42
Doppler, Christian, 13

E

Ettingshausen, Andreas von, 13

F

fertilization, 25, 28–30, 31, 44
feudalism, 15–17
Franz I, Emperor, 18
Franz, Friedrich, 10, 11

G

"*Gärtner's Versuche und Beobachtungen über die Bastarderzeugung im Pflanzenreich*" (Gärtner's Experiments and Observations of Hybridization in the Plant Kingdom), 25
genes, 36–42, 43–46, 47–51
gene therapy, 48–49
genetic modification, 51
genetics, laws of, 28–30, 31–34, 35, 36–42, 47, 49, 51

H

heredity, 4, 5, 20–22, 23–24, 36, 37–42, 47–49
Huntington's disease, 48
hybrids, 30, 31

I

identical twins, 44–46
Imperial Royal Gymnasium, 8–9

L

Lamarck, Jean-Baptiste, 20–21, 22

M

Mendel, Gregor
 abbot life, 34–35
 Augustinian monastery, 11, 17–19
 childhood, 6–10, 23
 education, 7–10, 13–14
 mathematical breakthrough, 31–32, 34
 pea experiments, 23–30, 31, 39–42
 priesthood, 10–11, 13, 17–19, 24–25
 teaching, 9–10, 11–13
Morgan, Thomas Hunt, 47
multiple sclerosis, 49

N

Naegeli, Karl Wilhelm von, 33–34
Napp, Abbot, 11, 13, 27
Natural History Society, 31–32
natural selection, 21–22
nucleus, 37

P

Parkinson's disease, 49
Philosophical Institute, 10

R

recessive genes, 37, 41–42

S

Schleiden, Matthias, 14
sex cells, 36–37, 39–40, 44–46

T

3:1 ratio, 29, 31, 37, 42
Truchsess-Zeil, Countess Walpurga, 16
Tschermak, Erich von, 35

U

Unger, Franz, 13–14
University of Vienna, 13–14, 24

V

"Versuche über Pflanzen-Hybriden," (Experiments on Plant Hybridization), 32–34

W

Watson, James, 47

Photo Credits

Cover, p. 20 © James King-Holmes/Science Photo Library; back cover: Copernicus image © Library of Congress Prints and Photographs Division, Darwin image © Library of Congress Prints and Photographs Division, Hubble image Courtesy Carnegie Observatories, The Carnegie Institution of Washington, Kepler image © Library of Congress Prints and Photographs Division, Mendel image © Pixtal/Superstock, Mendeleyev image © Edgar Fahs Smith Collection, University of Pennsylvania Library, Newton image © Library of Congress Prints and Photographs Division, Watson and Crick image © The James D. Watson Collection, Cold Spring Harbor Laboratory Archives; title page © Cynthia Hart Designer/Corbis; p. 5 © Hal Horwitz/Corbis; p. 7 © Bettmann/Corbis; p. 8 © Historical Picture Archive/Corbis; pp. 12, 18, 24, 26, 28, 32–33, 50 Stepan Bartos, Mendel Museum, Brno; p. 16 Steiermarkisches Landesmuseum Joanneum, Austria/Bridgeman Art Library; p. 21 Science, Industry and Business Library, The New York Public Library, Astor, Lenox, and Tilden Foundation; p. 27 Sheila Terry/Science Photo Library; p. 38 © Howard Sochurek/Corbis; p. 40 © Clouds Hill Imaging Ltd./Corbis; p. 43 John Kaprielian/Photo Researchers, Inc.; p. 45 © Photodisc; p. 46 © Jagadeesh Nv/Stringer/Reuters/Corbis; p. 48 © James King-Holmes/ICRF/Science Photo Library; p. 49 Time Life Pictures/Getty Images.

About the Author

Heather Elizabeth Hasan graduated college summa cum laude with a dual major in biochemistry and chemistry. She currently resides in Montgomery County, Maryland, with her husband, Omar, and their son, Samuel.

Editor: Nicholas Croce; Photo Researcher: Rebecca Anguin-Cohen